EXPERIMENT STATION
TUSKEGEE NORMAL AND INDUSTRIAL INSTITUTE
TUSKEGEE INSTITUTE, ALABAMA

HOW TO GROW

THE PEANUT

AND 105 WAYS OF PREPARING IT
FOR HUMAN CONSUMPTION

BY
G. W. CARVER, M. S. AGR,
DIRECTOR

Back cover photograph: George Washington Carver seated (front row, center) on steps at the Tuskegee Normal and Industrial Institute, with staff, ca. 1902. Library of Congress Prints and Photographs Division, LC-DIG-ppmsca-05633/ Frances Benjamin Johnston

Thank you for purchasing an Applewood book. Applewood reprints America's lively classics — books from the past that are still of interest to modern readers.

For all general information,
please contact Arcadia Publishing:
Telephone 843-853-2070
Fax 843-853-0044
E-mail sales@arcadiapublishing.com
For customer service and orders:
Toll-Free 1-888-313-2665

Visit us on the Internet at www.arcadiapublishing.com

978-1-4290-9686-7

MANUFACTURED IN THE UNITED STATES OF AMERICA
WITH AMERICAN-MADE MATERIALS

THE TUSKEGEE EXPERIMENT STATION

BOARD OF REGENTS

STATION STAFF

FOREWORD

In the preparation of this bulletin I wish to gratefully acknowledge assistance from the following sources, regretting that no credit can be given quite a number, as the information was obtained from clippings without the author's name:

Several Bulletins from the U. S. Department of Agriculture,
The Rural World,
The Rural New Yorker,
The Southern Ruralist,
Farm and Fireside,
The Country Gentleman,
The Kansas Farmer,
The Hearthstone,
Peerless Cook Book,
Home Cooking,
Common-Sense Recipes,
Royal Baker and Pastry Book,
The American Agriculturist,
The Tribune Farmer,
The Montgomery Advertiser,
The Farm and Home,
Berry's Fruit Recipes,
Wallaces' Farmer,
Leaflets from the West Virginia University,
The Rumford Book,
Bulletins from the University of Nebraska,
Several Leaflets from Cornell University.
Good Housekeeping.

NOTE. — Always remove the brown hull from the peanuts even though the recipe does not say so.

HOW TO GROW THE PEANUT

and 105 Ways of Preparing It for Human Consumption

Of all the money crops grown by Macon County farmers, perhaps there are none more promising than the peanut in its several varieties and their almost limitless possibilities.

Of the many good things in their favor, the following stand out as most prominent:

1. Like all other members of the pod-bearing family, they enrich the soil.

2. They are easily and cheaply grown.

3. For man the nuts possess a wider range of food values than any other legume.

4. The nutritive value of the hay as a stock food compares favorably with that of the cow pea.

5. They are easy to plant, easy to grow and easy to harvest.

6. The great food-and-forage value of the peanut will increase in proportion to the rapidity with which we make it a real study. This will increase consumption, and therefore, must increase production.

7. In this county two crops per year of the Spanish variety can be raised.

8. The peanut exerts a dietetic or a medicinal effect upon the human system that is very desirable.

9. I doubt if there is another foodstuff that can be so universally eaten, in some form, by every individual.

10. Pork fattened from peanuts and hardened off with a little corn just before killing, is almost if not quite equal to the famous Red-gravy hams or the world renowned Beech-nut breakfast bacon.

11. The nuts yield a high percentage of oil of superior quality.

12. The clean cake, after the oil has been removed, is very high in muscle-building properties (protein), and the ease with which the meal blends in with flour, meal, etc., makes it of especial value to bakers, confectioners, candy-makers, and ice cream factories.

13. Peanut oil is one of the best known vegetable oils.

14. A pound of peanuts contains a little more of the body-building nutrients than a pound of sirloin steak, while of the heat- and energy-producing nutrients it has more than twice as much.

VARIETIES

There are many varieties of the peanut, all possessing more or less merit. A number have been tested here on our Station grounds, and we can heartily recommend the following varieties in the order named:

1st, The Spanish. — As compared with most other varieties the vines are small, upright in growth, with nearly all the pods clinging close to the tap-root; hence, they can be planted closer together and the yield be larger.

This variety produced 59 bushels per acre on very light, sandy soil.

2nd, The Georgia Red and Tennessee Red. — These are practically one and the same variety — habit of growth and fruiting qualities much the same as the Spanish — with us it made a slightly lower yield.

This variety has from three to four kernels to the pod. The nuts are rich in flavor.

3rd, The Virginia Running Variety. — This variety is often referred to as the typical American peanut. It is decidedly the most popular with the trade. The pods are large and white, the vines spreading, and under . favorable conditions it fruits nearly out to the ends of the branches.

SOIL

With reference to soil there are two things to bear in mind; viz., whether they are for market or home consumption.

The trade demands a light-colored shell, which is only produced on light, sandy, porous soil.

More bushels per acre can be grown on stiff, clayey soil than upon light soil, but the pods will be stained dark. In fact any land that will produce good corn will produce good peanuts provided there is plenty of lime in it.

PREPARATION

In the preparation of the soil the chief essentials are —

1. Deep plowing, from 8 to 9 inches.

2. Thorough pulverization with a harrow, drag, smoothing board, etc.

3. Remove all stones, roots, stumps, clods, and obstructions of all kinds.

FERTILIZERS FOR PEANUTS

The peanut is an interesting plant, in that it adjusts itself to many kinds and methods of fertilization. It does well fertilized exactly as for corn; makes a splendid yield when given the same treatment as cow peas; does equally well when fertilized the same as for cotton.

For the sandy soils of Macon County we found the following compost mixture most satisfactory :

In the fall and winter a large pen was filled with leaves — muck from the swamp— and farmyard manure. The mixture consisted of one load of leaves from the woods together with the rich top earth, one load of muck from the swamp, and one load of manure from the barns, pig-pen, poultry house, etc. The pen was filled in this way, a rough shed put over it to throw off the excess of water, so the fertility would not be washed out. Eighteen tons of this mixture, together with 100 lbs. acid phosphate, 50 lbs. kainit, and 200 lbs. lime, were applied to the acre.

Where one must depend upon a commercial mixture the one given below gave decidedly the largest yield:

Acid phosphate . . . . .55 lbs.
Cotton-seed meal . . . . .125 lbs
Kainit . . . . .100 lbs.
Barnyard manure. . . . . 3 tons
Agricultural lime . . . . .200 lbs.

Note. — On soils containing lime, do not add any to the fertilizer mixture.

PLANTING

The time for planting the peanut in this locality is practically the same as for corn, beginning about the middle of March when not hulled, and the first of April when shelled. A good plan is to break the shell crosswise; they come up almost as quickly as when shelled.

If the Spanish peanut is shelled and planted early in April, it will mature about the middle of July, when they can be pulled, the ground prepared again, reseeded, and a second crop produced. There are two principal methods of planting the peanut; viz., in drills and checks. The drill method proved most desirable with us, giving the largest yield.

For the Spanish we placed our rows from 2½ to 3 feet apart; for the running varieties, from 3 to 3½ feet apart. Furrows were run as nearly 4 inches deep as possible, the compost put directly into the furrow, and the nuts planted on it.

CULTIVATION

If the land has been well prepared as above directed and is practically free from weed seeds, the cultivation will be quite simple. Cultivate only enough to keep the ground soft and mellow and free from weeds.

There are two methods, however, of cultivating the peanut; viz., the ridge method, and the flat method. We tried both, and the flat .method gave decidedly the best results.

HARVESTING

The time to harvest varies with the date of planting and the variety of peanut. Experienced planters prefer to get their crop harvested before the first killing frost, because it not only injures some of the nuts, but greatly damages the hay, by lowering its feeding value and causing the vines to drop their leaves.

There are a number of special plows and devices made to render harvesting of the crop as easy as possible. All of them have more or less merit. The small farmer, however, can use to good advantage the same method used in harvesting the sweet potato; viz., that of plowing a furrow on each side of the vines, and then bursting out the middle containing vines, which can be picked up readily, the earth shaken off and the vines wind-rowed, loosely piled, or treated in any way desired. An old and favorite way is to plow up the vines in the morning of a warm, sunshiny day, allowing them to dry until late in the afternoon, when they are gathered up and stacked around poles, which are about 7 feet high, and set firmly in the ground at convenient places over the field.

Logs or poles should be laid on the ground around the center pole, so as to keep the vines off the ground. Stack loosely so the air can pass through freely. Care should be taken to stack the vines so the peanuts will be on the inside next the pole.

Cap the stacks with hay, straw, corn stalks, or anything that will turn the water. If the weather is good they may be safely picked, in from 15 to 20 days after stacking.

PICKING

There are so many good pickers on the market now, together with a great many simple and effective home-made devices, that I think any further mention of them would be wholly out of place.

PREPARATION FOR MARKET

Peanuts, like everything else, sell more quickly and bring a better price if the nuts are uniform in size, clean, and the shells of a bright color. If washing is necessary, it should be done on a clear, warm day, and they should be dried quickly in the sun.

A large number of the pops and otherwise faulty nuts can be removed by winnowing them in a good, strong wind, like peas. They should now he put in bags holding 100 lbs. each.

Put away in a dry, well-ventilated house until ready to sell. The pops and faulty nuts can be fed to the hogs.

PEANUT HAY

Hay made from peanut vines, like all our cultivated pod-bearing plants, possesses high feeding value. The following table, from the best known authorities, shows it as compared with alfalfa, cow-pea vines, crimson and burr clover (air-dried material):

NAME	WATER	CRUDE ASH	PROTEIN MUSCLE-BUILDERS	CRUDE FIBER	FATS	CARBOHY-DRATES FAT-FORMERS
Peanut	7.83%	17.04%	11.75%	22.11%	1.84%	46.95%
Alfalfa	6.95%	7.49%	16.48%	31.38%	2.03%	42.62%
Cow-Pea Vines	10.29%	9.10%	19.72%	21.99%	4.04%	45.15%
Crimson Clover	9.60%	8.60%	15.20%	27.20%	2.80%	36.60%
Red Clover	14.30%	7.47%	12.84%	29.27%	2.11%	48.31%

It is readily seen by the above table that peanut hay compares very favorably with the much-prized market hays of superior feeding value. One and one-fourth tons of cured hay was produced on an acre in our Station, in addition to the 59 bushels of nuts.

AS A FOOD FOR MAN

By reason of its superior food value the peanut has become almost a universal diet for man, and when we learn its real value, I think I am perfectly safe in the assertion that it will not only become a prime essential in every well-balanced dietary, but a real necessity. Indeed, I do not know of any one vegetable that has such a wide range of food possibilities.

Below are given 105 ways of preparing the peanut for human consumption, with the hope that every farmer will learn to appreciate them and raise large quantities for his own consumption; and also with the hope that the city folk will find the diet not only wholesome, satisfying, healthful and appetizing, but very economical. Fourteen recipes were selected from this number, and a five course luncheon served to ten food specialists; and each one without exception was enthusiastic over it, and said it was the most satisfying luncheon he or she had ever eaten.

A glance at the table below is sufficient to impress anyone most favorably with the superior value of the peanut as a food:

FOOD	WATER	PROTEIN (MUSCLE-BUILDERS)	CARBOHYDRATES (FAT-FORMERS)
Peanut	9.2%	25.8%	63.0%
Boston Beans	12.6%	22.5%	59.6%
Cow-Pea	13.0%	21.4%	60.8%

No. 1— PEANUT SOUP

One quart milk
2 tablespoonfuls butter
2 tablespoonfuls flour
1 cup peanuts.

Cook peanuts until soft; remove skins, mash or grind until very fine; let milk come to a boil; add the peanuts; cook 20 minutes.

Rub flour into a smooth paste with milk; add butter to the peanuts and milk; stir in flour; season with salt and pepper to taste; serve hot.

No. 2, PEANUT SOUP NUMBER TWO

Take roasted peanuts; grind or mash real fine; to every half a pint add a quart of hot milk, half a teaspoon salt, 1 saltspoon pepper, 1 small onion minced very fine, 1 bay leaf, 1 stalk celery chopped very fine or a saltspoon celery seed. Cook for 15 minutes. Great care must be exercised to keep it from burning.

Moisten 1 tablespoon of corn starch in a quarter cup of cold milk; add to the soup; stir until thick and smooth; strain through a fine sieve, and serve with peanut wafers.

No. 3, PEANUT BISQUE

To 3 cups of boiling milk add half teaspoon chopped onion, a pinch of salt and pepper; rub to a smooth paste a tablespoon of flour with water; add half cup of peanut butter; stir in the flour; boil 3 minutes longer; serve with peanut wafers.

No. 4, PEANUT SOUP NUMBER FOUR

Boil 10 minutes in half a cup of water, half a cup chopped celery, a tablespoon of chopped onion, the same amount of red and green peppers mixed; add a cup of peanut butter and 3 cups of rich milk to which has been added 1 tablespoon of flour; add 1 teaspoon of sugar; boil two minutes and serve.

No. 5, CONSOMME OF PEANUTS

Take 1 pint of shelled peanuts; boil or steam until the skins can be removed; boil in salted water until tender and until nearly all the water boils away; add 1 quart of beef stock, a few grains of cayenne, half a teaspoon salt; let boil slowly for 10 minutes; serve hot.

No. 6, PUREE OF PEANUTS

1 pint of peanuts, blanched and ground,
1 pint milk,
½ cup cream,
1 tablespoon butter,
1 egg, well beaten.

Let the milk and cream come to a boil; stir in all the other ingredients; add more milk if too thick; salt and pepper to taste; serve at once with peanut wafers.

No. 7, PUREE OF PEANUTS NUMBER TWO (EXTRA FINE)

Take 1 pint of peanuts; roast until the shells rub off easily (do not brown); grind very fine; add a saltspoon of salt, 1 teaspoon sugar; pour on boiling water, and stir until thick as cream. Set in double boiler and boil from 8 to 10 hours; set away and allow to get thoroughly cold; turn out. Can be eaten hot or cold. When sliced, rolled in bread crumbs or cracker dust and fried a chicken brown, it makes an excellent substitute for meat.

A generous layer between slices of bread makes an excellent sandwich.

No. 8, PEANUT BREAD NUMBER ONE

Into any good biscuit dough work in a liberal supply of blanched and ground nuts; roll out thin; cut in small discs, and bake in a quick oven; serve hot.

No. 9, PEANUT BREAD NUMBER TWO

½ cupful sugar,
2 teaspoons baking powder,
½ cupful blanched and chopped nuts,
½ cupful sweet milk,
1 egg, beat in,
2 cupfuls sifted flour.

Mix these ingredients; make into small loaves or biscuits; let rise for one-half hour; bake in a slow oven until done, which will require about 50 minutes.

No. 10, ENGLISH PEANUT BREAD

2 cups liquid yeast,
1 tablespoon butter,
2 tablespoons sugar,
1 teaspoon of salt.

Flour as long as you can stir it with a spoon; beat it long and hard; let stand in a warm place over night; in the morning add one cup of blanched and finely-chopped peanuts; add flour to make a soft dough; let stand in a warm place until light; bake in a moderate oven one hour.

No. 11, AUNT NELLIE'S PEANUT BROWN BREAD

1½ cups white flour,
1½ cups Graham flour,
2 teaspoons baking powder,
½ cup sweet milk, or just enough
   to make a soft dough,
1 teaspoon salt,
½ cup blanched and ground peanuts.

Mix well together and bake in a moderate oven.

No. 12, OATMEAL PEANUT BREAD (DELICIOUS)

2 cups liquid yeast,
2 cups rolled oats,
2 teaspoons sugar,
1 teaspoon salt,
1 tablespoon butter.

Add white flour as long as you can stir it; beat well; let rise over night; stir up well in the morning; add one cup of chopped or ground peanuts; pour into buttered baking-pan and set in a warm place to rise; when light bake in a moderate oven for one hour.

No. 13, PEANUT BREAD NUMBER THREE

A delicious loaf can be made by adding half a pint of finely-ground nuts to every loaf of bread when baking. Add the nuts when the bread is worked down the last time.

No. 14, PEANUT ROLLS NUMBER ONE

2 cups of soft, white bread-crumbs,
4 tablespoons peanut butter,
½ cupful grated cocoanut, chopped fine,
1 saltspoon celery seed,
1 teaspoon salt,
1 well-beaten egg,
½ pound blanched and ground peanuts.

Mix thoroughly; make into rolls, and fry in deep fat or bake in an oven; serve with nut sauce.

No. 15, PEANUT ROLLS NUMBER TWO

Make the dough exactly the same as for Parker House rolls. At the last working add a heaping teaspoon of ground peanuts, and work into each roll.

No. 16, SWEDISH NUT ROLLS

1 pint milk, scalded,
½ cup butter,
¼ cup sugar,
1 scant teaspoon salt,
2 eggs (whites),
½ cup yeast, 7 or 8 cups flour.

Mix early in the morning a sponge with the milk, sugar, salt, eggs, and yeast, using flour enough to make a drop batter. Place in a pan of warm water, and when light add the butter (softened) and enough more flour to thicken it. Knead well, and let it rise again. When light roll out into a large triangular piece one-third of an inch thick. Spread all over with soft butter and a sprinkling of sugar, cinnamon, and a generous coating of finely-ground peanuts. Roll over and over; cut off slices an inch thick; lay them on a well-buttered pan with the cut-side down. Let it rise again, and bake in a moderate oven.

No. 17, PEANUT COOKIES NUMBER ONE

3 cups flour,
2 eggs,
1 cup sugar,
1½ cups ground peanuts,
½ cup butter,
1 cup sweet milk,
1 teaspoon baking powder.

Cream butter and sugar; add eggs well beaten; now add the milk and flour; flavor to taste with vanilla; add the peanuts last; drop one spoonful to the cooky in well-greased pans; bake quickly.

No. 18, PEANUT COOKIES NUMBER TWO

4 teaspoons butter,
1 cup sugar,
2 eggs, well-beaten,
2 teaspoons baking powder,
2 cups flour,
1 cup ground peanuts,

Sweet milk sufficient to make a stiff batter. Drop on well-greased tins and bake quickly.

No. 19, PEANUT COOKIES NUMBER THREE

One-third cup butter,
½ cup sugar,
2 eggs well beaten,
½ cup flour,
1 teaspoon baking powder,
1 cup blanched and finely-chopped peanuts,
1 teaspoon lemon juice.

Sweet milk enough to make a stiff batter. Cream the butter, and add the sugar and eggs well beaten. Sift the flour and baking powder together. Add the butter, sugar, eggs, and flour; then add the milk, nuts, and lemon juice. Drop from a spoon on an unbuttered baking sheet; sprinkle with chopped nuts, and bake in a very slow oven.

No. 20, PEANUT TEA ROLLS (DELICIOUS)

2 cups raised sponge,
1 cup sugar,
½ cup butter,
1 cup ground peanuts.

Take two cups of sponge, the sugar, melted butter, eggs, peanuts, and salt to taste. Mix thoroughly; knead in enough flour to make dough as for rolls. Set in a warm place to rise; when light shape into rolls; let rise until twice their size; rub melted butter over the top with a small paint brush; then sift sugar and ground peanuts over the top.

No. 21, PEANUT BARS

2 cups flour,
1 cup coarsely-chopped peanuts,
½ cup sugar,
2 tablespoons butter,
1 teaspoon baking powder,
½ cup milk,
1 egg,
Pinch of salt.

Sift flour, salt, and baking powder into a bowl; rub in the butter, nuts, and sugar; mix to a rather stiff dough with the egg and milk; turn on to a floured board, and roll out two-thirds of an inch thick; cut into bars of convenient size, and fry in the fat until ^ golden brown.

No. 22, PEANUT WAFERS NUMBER ONE

2 cups flour,
1 cup water,
1 cup sugar (powdered),
½ cup rolled peanuts,
½ cup butter.

Rub the butter and sugar together until light and creamy; add the flour and water alternately. Lastly add the peanuts; drop on buttered tins, and bake quickly. Cut in squares while hot, as it soon gets brittle after cooling.

No. 23, PEANUT WAFERS NUMBER TWO

¼ cup butter,
1 cup flour,
1 cup sugar,
1 cup blanched nuts,
1 egg.

Grind or roll the nuts; stir into the butter; drop on buttered tins, and bake quickly.

No. 24, PEANUT WAFERS NUMBER THREE

3 tablespoons flour,
½ teaspoon baking powder,
2 well-beaten eggs,
½ lb. brown sugar,
1 cupful ground peanuts.

Mix thoroughly; drop on buttered paper, and bake slowly to a light brown.

No. 25, PEANUT MUFFINS NUMBER ONE

½ cupful chopped peanuts,
2 eggs beaten very light,
½ teaspoon soda, dissolved in
    tablespoon of water,
½ pint thick sour buttermilk,
½ teaspoon salt,
1½ cupfuls flour, or enough to
    make a stiff batter.

Add soda to the sour milk; stir well; make the batter quickly; when ready to drop into the pans add peanuts; bake in a quick oven from 26 to 25 minutes.

No. 26, PEANUT MUFFINS NUMBER TWO

Use the above recipe, and in addition add Y 2 cupful of cold, cooked rice. Chopped figs, dates, etc., make very pleasing variations.

No. 27, PEANUT DOUGHNUTS NUMBER ONE

2 eggs, beaten light,
1 cup sugar,
3 tablespoons melted butter,
1 cup sour milk,
4 cups flour,
½ teaspoon soda,
1 saltspoon salt,
1 saltspoon cinnamon,
1 cup finely-ground or
    chopped peanuts.

Into the well-beaten eggs stir the sugar, butter, milk, and nuts; add flour to make a dough just stiff enough to roll out; roll, cut out, and fry in deep fat hot enough for the dough to rise at once.

No. 28, PEANUT DOUGHNUTS NUMBER TWO

1 pint sweet milk,
1 cup sugar,
½ cup butter (softened),
Two-thirds cup yeast,
1 egg, well beaten,
1 tablespoon lemon juice,
5½ to 6 cups flour,
1 pint chopped peanuts.

Mix in the order given; rise slowly till light; roll out and cut in shape; rise quickly until very light, then fry in hot fat.

CAKES

No. 29, PEANUT CAKE NUMBER ONE

¼ lb. butter,
2 cups flour,
4 eggs (whites only) well beaten,
¾ cup water,
1 cup finely-ground peanuts,
1 teaspoon baking powder.

Beat the sugar and butter to a cream; add the water and flour; stir until/ smooth; add half the well-beaten whites, then the nuts, then the remainder of the whites and the baking power; pour into square, flat pans lined with greased paper to the depth of three inches, and bake in a moderate oven for 45 or 50 minutes.

No. 30, PEANUT CAKE NUMBER TWO

9 ounces flour,
4 ounces butter,
4 ounces chopped peanuts,
4 eggs,
1 teaspoon vanilla,
¼ teaspoon salt,
1 teaspoon baking powder.

Sift flour, salt, and baking powder together; cream the butter and sugar; add the vanilla, chopped nuts, and yolks of the eggs well beaten; add flour, then whipped whites, and beat well; bake in shallow pan in medium oven; when cold, ice with boiled icing.

No. 31, PEANUT ROLL CAKE WITH JELLY

4 eggs,
Two-third cup powdered sugar,
Two-third cup flour,
¼ teaspoon salt,
½ teaspoon baking powder.

Beat egg yolks and sugar till light; add mixed dry ingredients, then stiffly beaten whites; mix lightly together. Bake in thin sheet in a quick oven. As soon as done turn quickly on a towel wrung out of water; spread with jelly; sprinkle liberally with coarsely-chopped peanuts; roll up and dust with powdered sugar.

No. 32, PEANUT LAYER CAKE

Make cake exactly the same as for roll cake, except bake in jelly-cake tins. Make the pastry cream as follows:

2 cups sugar,
1½ pints milk,
3 tablespoons corn starch,
1 tablespoon butter,
2 teaspoons extract of lemon,
1 pint coarsely-ground peanuts.

Add peanuts to the milk; let simmer 5 minutes; with sugar add the starch dissolved in a little cold water; as soon as it reboils take from the fire; beat in the yolks; return to the fire two or three minutes to set the eggs; when cold spread between the layers of cake, and finish with clear icing garnished with blanched peanuts.

No. 33, METROPOLITAN CAKE WITH PEANUTS

1 cup granulated sugar,
1½ cups butter,
½ cup milk,
2½ cups well-sifted flour,
2 teaspoons baking powder,
  sifted with the flour,
1 cupful chopped peanuts
  and citron mixed,
4 eggs (whites).

Cream the butter and sugar; flour nuts and citron before adding; bake 45 minutes in a moderate oven; flavor icing with lemon extract, and garnish top with split peanuts and pecan meats.

No. 34, PEANUT CAKE WITH MOLASSES

2 cups molasses,
1 cup brown sugar,
1 cup lard,
2 cups hot water,
4 cups flour,
1 pint ground peanuts,
2 teaspoons cinnamon,
½ teaspoon cloves,
¼ of a nutmeg, grated,
1 heaping teaspoon soda,
1 egg.

Mix the peanuts, spices, and soda with the flour; heap the measure of flour slightly; mix the molasses, sugar, lard, and water; stir in the flour; add the beaten egg last. Bake in shallow dripping-pan, and sprinkle with powdered sugar just before putting in the oven.

No. 35, PEANUT PUDDING

1 cup molasses,
½ cup butter,
1 cup hot water,
3 cups flour,
1 teaspoon soda,
½ cup coarsely-ground peanuts,
½ teaspoon ground cloves.

Mix, and steam two hours. Sauce for same:

1 tablespoon butter,
½ cup sugar,
1 teaspoon flour,

Mix all to a cream; pour over this enough boiling water to make it like cream; flavor to suit the taste.

No. 36, PEANUT STRIPS WITH BANANAS

2 cups mashed banana pulp,
1 cup oat flakes,
1 cup flour,
1 cup peanut meal,
1 cup sugar,
½ cup butter (softened).
1 saltspoon (or more) of salt.

Blend all together; roll out ¼ of an inch thick; cut in strips, and bake in a quick oven.

MISCELLANEOUS DISHES FROM PEANUTS

No. 37, LIVER WITH PEANUTS

Boil the livers from two fowl or a turkey; when tender mash them fine; boil one pint of blanched peanuts until soft; mash them to a smooth paste; mix, and rub through a puree-strainer; season to taste with salt, pepper, and lemon juice; moisten with melted butter; spread the paste on bread like sandwiches, or add enough hot chicken stock to make a puree; heat again and season with salt, pepper, and lemon juice.

No. 38, MOCK CHICKEN

Blanch and grind a sufficient number of peanuts until they are quite oily; stir in one well-beaten egg; if too thin, thicken with rolled bread crumbs or cracker dust; stir in little salt. Boil some sweet potatoes until done; peel and cut in thin slices; spread generously with the peanut mixture; dip in white of egg; fry to a chicken brown; serve hot.

No. 39, MOCK VEAL CUTLETS

Wash one cup of lentils, and soak over night; in the morning strain and parboil in fresh boiling water for 30 minutes; drain again, and cook until soft in sufficient boiling water to cover them; rub through a sieve, and to the puree add hi cup of melted butter, 1 cup of fine Graham bread crumbs, 1 cup of strained tomatoes to which a speck of soda has been added, 1 cup of blanched and chopped peanuts, 1 tablespoon each of grated celery and minced onion ; season with ¼ teaspoon of mixed herbs, salt, and pepper; blend all thoroughly together, and form into cutlets; dip these in egg and then in fine bread-crumbs; place in a well-greased baking pan, and brown in quick oven; arrange around a mound of well-seasoned mashed potatoes, and serve with brown sauce.

No. 40, PEANUT PATTIES

1 pint toasted bread crumbs rolled fine,
1 pint mashed potatoes (white or sweet),
2 teaspoons baking powder dissolved in the yolks
    of two eggs,

Season with salt, pepper, sage, and mace; heat all together; form into small cakes; dip each cake into the whites of the eggs, then into peanut meal, and brown lightly in a frying-pan containing a little pork fat, not deep fat; turn and brown on both sides.

No. 41, BROWN SAUCE

Mix thoroughly 1 teaspoon of peanut butter and 2 tablespoons browned flour with 1 tablespoon cream; add gradually 2 cups hot milk, and stir and cook until the mixture thickens; just before serving add 4 tablespoons strained tomatoes, and a little salt and pepper.

PEANUT SAUSAGES

Grind ½ pound of roasted peanuts, ½ pound pecans, 1 ounce hickory nuts, and ½ pound walnut meats. Mix with six very ripe bananas; pack in a mould, and steam continuously for two hours; when done remove lid of kettle or mould, and when mixture is cold turn out and serve the same as roast meat sliced thin for sandwiches, or with cold tomato sauce or other sauce.

No. 43, PEANUT AND CHEESE ROAST

1 cup grated cheese,
1 cup finely-ground peanuts,
1 cup bread crumbs,
1 teaspoon chopped onion,
1 tablespoon butter,
Juice of half a lemon,
Salt and pepper to taste.

Cook the onion In the butter and a little water until it is tender. Mix the other ingredients, and moisten with water, using the water in which the onion has been cooked. Pour into a shallow' baking dish, and brown in the oven.

No. 44, PEANUT OMELET

Cream a slice of bread in half a cup of rich milk; beat the whites and yolks of two eggs separately; add the yolks to the bread-crumbs and milk; to half a cup of finely-ground peanuts add a dash of pepper and salt; mix thoroughly; fold in the whites, and cook as usual in a buttered pan.

No. 45, BAKED PEANUTS WITH RICE

4 cups milk,
One-third cup rice,
1 cup coarsely-ground peanuts,
One-third cup sugar,
1 tablespoon lemon juice,
½ teaspoon salt,

Wash rice, putting a layer of rice and a layer of peanuts into a well-buttered pudding-dish until all is used; mix the salt and sugar, sprinkling each layer with it; finish with a layer of peanuts on top, pour on the milk, if it does not cover the rice put in sufficient water; bake three hours in a very slow oven; add hot water if it cooks too dry.

No. 46, PEANUT MACARONI AND CHEESE

1 cup broken macaroni,
2 quarts boiling salted water,
1 cup rich milk,
2 tablespoons flour,
¼ to ½ pound cheese,
½ teaspoon salt,
1 cup coarsely ground peanuts,
A dash of cayenne pepper.

Cook macaroni in the boiling salted water; drain in a strainer, and pour cold water over it to keep the pieces from sticking together; mince cheese, and mix with all other ingredients except the macaroni; put sauce and macaroni in alternate layers in a well-buttered baking dish; cover with buttered crumbs, and bake slowly until crumbs are brown.

No. 47, PEANUT PIE-CRUST

Add at the rate of 1 tablespoon of finely-ground peanuts to one pie crust. You will be pleased with the agreeable change in pie-crusts or any other pastry.

No. 48, PEANUT BREAKFAST CAKES

Mash 2 cups of well-cooked, split peas or beans; press through a sieve; add 1 teaspoon grated celery, 1 teaspoon minced onion, 1 cup of milk, 1 cup softened bread crumbs, 1 tablespoon butter, 1 cup crushed peanuts, 1 well-beaten egg; season with salt and pepper; form into small flat cakes, and brown in hot fat; place a nicely-poached egg on each cake; garnish with parsley, and serve with hot cream or brown sauce.

No. 49, PEANUTS AND MUSHROOMS

Cook 2 tablespoons of chopped onion and ½ cup chopped fresh mushrooms in 4 tablespoons of butter for five or six minutes; stir in 2 tablespoons flour, a little salt and pepper, and 1½ cups milk; cook and stir the whole for five minutes longer; then add 1 cup finely-chopped peanuts; re-heat, and boil slowly for 10 minutes; serve on squares of buttered toast.

No. 50, PEANUT TIMBALES

½ pint of peanuts cooked until soft in salted water;
   drain and mash,
2 well-beaten eggs and two cups thin cream,
   added to the nuts,
½ teaspoon salt, and a dash of pepper,

Turn into custard cups; put the cups in a basin; surround them with boiling water; cover the tops With buttered paper, and bake in a moderate oven for 20 or 25 minutes; then unmould and serve with a little cream sauce poured around them.

No. 51, PEANUT BUTTER

Shell the peanuts; roast just enough so that the hulls will slip off easily; remove all the hulls by gently rolling, fanning, and screening; grind very fine in any sort of mill, passing through several times if necessary; pack in cans, bottles, or jars, and seal if not for immediate use. Some manufacturers add a little salt and a small amount of olive oil; others do not, according to taste. For small quantities of butter a good meat-grinder will answer the purpose. If the nuts are ground fine enough no additional oil will be necessary.

STUFFINGS

No. 52, PEANUT STUFFING NUMBER ONE

Crumble a pint of corn bread, adding to it a grated rind of one lemon, a cup of finely-chopped peanuts, two tablespoons of mixed, dried herbs, salt and pepper to taste, and one-half cup of melted butter. Bacon drippings may be used instead of butter.

No. 53, PEANUT STUFFING NUMBER TWO

½ pint shelled and roasted peanuts
   (peanut meal can be used),
4 drops onion juice,
1 teaspoon chopped parsley, slightly
   moistened with cream,
½ teaspoon powdered herbs.

Season highly with salt and pepper.

No. 54, PEANUT STUFFING NUMBER THREE

2 cups hot mashed potatoes,
1 teaspoon onion juice or grated onion,
½ cup ground peanuts
   (peanut meal is excellent),
¼ teaspoon paprika,
1 teaspoon salt,
4 tablespoons thick cream,
1 tablespoon butter,
2 eggs (yolks).

One teaspoon of sweet herbs if desired. Blend all together, and stuff in the usual way.

No. 55, PEANUT MEAL NUMBER ONE

Blanch the peanuts and grind very fine but not sufficient to become too oily. This meal is especially fine as a substitute in making almond macroons and small cakes, to which it imparts the desired almond flavor, and is much cheaper than the almond meal.

No. 56, BROWN PEANUT MEAL

Roast the peanuts carefully without scorching; when a rich light-brown rub off the hulls and grind the same as for No. 49. This meal has many uses, such as soups, gravies, cakes, candies, etc., etc.

No. 57, CREAM PEANUTS

1 pint white crowder peas,
1 cup cream,
1 pint peanuts,
1 teaspoon sugar,
½ teaspoon pepper,
1 saltspoon salt.

Boil the peas until thoroughly done; pass through a colander; grind or crush the blanched peanuts; add all the ingredients except the cream and nuts; boil thirty minutes; mix the cream and nuts together with a tablespoon of flour; mix thoroughly; stir into the boiling peas; boil five minutes; whip vigorously until light, and serve. If one spoonful of flour is not sufficient add more.

No. 58, SALTED PEANUTS

Roast the peanuts; shell, and remove the thin hulls; put in a pan; butter slightly; put in oven and heat through; spread on piece of white paper; sprinkle with fine salt, and serve.

Note. — If the nuts are very greasy allow them to drain before applying the salt.

No. 59, PEANUT BUTTER SANDWICHES

Roast the desired number of peanuts; rub the thin hull off the nuts; grind or rub in a mortar until quite smooth and oily; salt to taste, and spread a thin layer between crackers, lunch biscuits, rolls, or bread of that character. If the butter is not as thin as you wish add a little fresh cow's butter, a little milk or water, and rub well. This butter will not keep as well as when the milk or water is left out.

SALADS

No. 60, PEANUT SALAD NUMBER ONE

1 small cabbage,
1 teaspoon flour,
2 teaspoons salt,
1 teaspoon mustard,
1 teaspoon sugar,
1 cup vinegar,
1 teaspoon butter,
½ teaspoon pepper,
2 eggs,
1 pint peanuts.

Chop cabbage and peanuts up fine; add the salt and pepper; cream the butter, mustard, sugar, and flour together; stir in the vinegar; cook in double boiler until stiff; add yolks of the eggs; pour over nuts and cabbage, and serve.

No. 61, PEANUT SALAD NUMBER TWO

1 cup roasted peanuts,
1 cup sour apples.

Chop the nuts and apples together. Make a dressing of —

½ cup water,
½ cup sugar,
2 tablespoons butter,
½ cup vinegar,
1 tablespoon flour,
1 egg.

Whip all together, and let boil long enough to thicken; then pour over salad; serve on crisp lettuce leaves.

No. 62, PEANUT SALAD NUMBER THREE

Blanch peanuts; put in the oven and brown with a bit of butter and a sprinkle of salt; when cold chop coarsely. To each cupful of nuts add two cups of finely-shredded celery and an equal amount of sour apples; mix thoroughly; serve on lettuce leaves with mayonnaise dressing.

No. 63, PEANUT AND DATE SALAD

2 cups dates, stoned and cut into small pieces,
½ cup coarsely-ground peanuts,
2 cups celery, finely cut.

Stir well, then mix with cream salad dressing.

No. 64, PEANUT SALAD WITH BANANAS

Slice bananas through center; spread out on lettuce leaves, and sprinkle liberally with chopped peanuts ; serve with mayonnaise or plain salad dressing.

ICE CREAM

No. 65, PEANUT ICE CREAM NUMBER ONE

1 pint peanuts,
2 quarts milk,
2 cups sugar,
1 pint cream,
3 eggs,
2 teaspoons vanilla.

Roast, shell, and roll the peanuts until they are quite fine; brown one cup of sugar and add to the milk; next add remainder of sugar, the cream, vanilla, and lastly the peanuts; freeze.

No. 66, PEANUT CREAM NUMBER TWO

Make a quart of lemon or vanilla cream by the usual rule; when this is half frozen take out the dasher and add ½ pound of peanut brittle, or two or three bars of peanut candy previously put through the meat chopper. The result is a light-brown cream tasting: like caramel, with the nuts all through it. It may be served in glasses or put in a brick.

No. 67, PEANUT CREAM (PROFESSIONAL WAY)

Take 21 pounds of 18 per cent cream, 4 pounds granulated sugar. 1 teaspoon peanut butter dissolved in ½ cup boiling water; add caramel to give the light-brown hue desired; freeze in the ordinary way.

This gives only a pleasing suggestion of peanut flavor. If more is desired increase the quantity of butter or add peanut meal.

No. 68, PEANUT FRAPPE

Make 1 pint of good gelatine; set aside to harden. Stir 1 cup granulated sugar into 1 pint of whipped cream; when the gelatine is just on the point of setting stir into it the whipped cream by beating with a fork; add ¾ cup of peanut meal; serve in sherbet glasses with fresh or preserved fruit.

No. 69, PEANUT AND PRUNE ICE CREAM

2 cups milk,
3 eggs (yolks),
½ pound pulp from well-cooked & sweetened prunes,
1 quart cream,
½ cup blanched and ground peanuts.
   (Peanut meal can be used),
1 teaspoon vanilla extract and a pinch of salt.

Heat the milk; pour it into the well-beaten egg yolks; blend all the other ingredients thoroughly; freeze and serve in dainty glasses.

CANDIES AND CONFECTIONS

No. 70, PEANUT-BUTTER CANDY

2 cups sugar,
½ cup milk,
2 tablespoons peanut butter.

Blend together; boil for five minutes; remove from the fire and beat steadily until cool.

No. 71, PEANUT CANDY

2 cups sugar,
1 cup peanuts.

Melt the sugar in a frying pan; melt slowly, stirring constantly until melted; butter a shallow dish, and cover bottom with the roasted and cleaned nuts; pour the candy over them; set aside; when cool break in pieces, and serve.

No. 72, PEANUT CARAMELS

1 cup sugar,
1 cup molasses,
1 cup butter,
1 cup milk or cream,
1 cup ground peanuts.

Cream sugar and butter; add molasses, cream or milk, stirring constantly; put mixture into a boiler and let boil, gently scraping the bottom to prevent burning (do not stir); let cook until it forms a soft mass when dropped into cool water; add peanuts and pour into buttered tins. The layer should not be more than ½ an inch thick. When cool enough cut into small squares, and wrap in thin glazed paper.

No. 73, PEANUT KISSES

1 egg (white),
1 cupful sifted brown sugar,
1 cupful chopped peanuts,
¼ teaspoon vanilla.

Beat the egg-white very stiff; stir in the sugar, nuts, and vanilla, and drop on a buttered pan; make the kisses two inches apart; bake in a moderate oven.

No. 74, PEANUT CHOCOLATE TAFFY

½ pound of sweet chocolate,
2 cups granulated sugar,
¼ teaspoon cream of tartar,
½ cup boiling water,
½ cup of peanut meal or coarsely-ground meats, as
    desired.

Grate the chocolate; add the boiling water; stir until dissolved. Place the kettle over the fire, and cook for several minutes; add the peanuts, and boil until the candy will snap when pulled apart; remove from the fire, and pour out to cool; pull and cut as desired.

No. 75, PEANUT BALLS

2 cups brown sugar,
1 cup New Orleans molasses,
½ cup water,
¼ (scant) teaspoon cream of tartar.

Boil all together until the candy will snap when tested in cold water; remove from the fire; add two cups blanched peanuts (coarsely broken); stir until nearly cold; form into balls by rolling between palms of the hands; wrap in paraffin paper to prevent sticking together.

No. 76, PEANUT CANDY NUMBER TWO

2 cups brown sugar,
1 cup rich milk,
¼ cup syrup,
1 tablespoon butter,
1 cup shelled peanuts.

Mix sugar, syrup, milk, and butter; boil until a soft ball can be formed by dropping in cold water; when nearly cold beat, and add nuts.

No. 77, PEANUT FILLING
FOR CAKES, COOKIES, ETC.

3 teaspoons corn starch,
2 eggs (yolks),
½ cup rich milk,
½ cup sugar,
1 cup chopped peanut meats,
½ cup water.

Use double boiler; put in the water and milk; when hot stir in 3 teaspoons corn starch previously dissolved in a little cold, water; cook for 10 minutes; add the beaten yolks of 2 eggs that have been creamed with ½ cup sugar; cook for 3 minutes; when cold add the chopped nuts; flavor with lemon or vanilla.

No. 78, CANDIED PEANUTS

....

3 cups sugar,
1 cup water.

Boil until it hardens when dropped in water; then flavor with lemon. It must not boil after the lemon is put in. Put a nut on end of a fine knitting-needle; dip; take out and turn until cold. If the candy gets cold set on a warm stove for a few minutes.

No. 79, PEANUT NOUGAT WITH HONEY

....

3/8 cup honey,
½ cup brown sugar,
1 pound blanched peanuts,
2 eggs (whites).

Boil the honey and sugar together until drops of the mixture hold their shape when poured into cold water; add whites of the two eggs, well beaten, and cook very slowly, stirring constantly until the mixture becomes brittle when dropped in cold water; add the peanuts and cool under a weight; break in pieces or cut and wrap in waxed paper.

No. 80, PEANUT BUTTER FUDGE

2 cups powdered sugar,
1 cup milk,
2 heaping teaspoons peanut butter.

Mix ingredients; boil vigorously five minutes; beat; pour in a buttered pan, and cut in squares.

No. 81, PEANUT DIVINITY FUDGE

2½ cups sugar,
½ cup syrup,
½ cup water,
2 eggs,
1 cup coarsely-broken peanuts.

Boil the sugar, syrup, and water together until, when dropped in -cold water, the mixture will form a hard ball between the fingers; beat the eggs stiff; pour half the boiling mixture over eggs, beating constantly; return remaining half of the mixture to the stove, and boil until it forms a hard ball when dropped into cold water; remove from the stove, and pour slowly into first half, beating constantly; add peanuts, and flavor with vanilla; pour into a buttered pan, and cut into squares.

No. 82, PEANUT CHOCOLATE FUDGE

2 cups white granualated sugar,
1 tablespoon butter,
1 cup cream,
¼ cake unsweetened chocolate,
I cup chopped peanuts.

Put in the sugar and cream, and when this becomes hot put in the chocolate, broken up into fine pieces ; stir vigorously and constantly, put in the butter when it begins to boil; stir until it creams when beaten on a saucer; remove and beat until quite cool, and pour into buttered tins; add the nuts before stirring.

No. 83, PEANUT BRITTLE NUMBER ONE

3 cups granulated sugar,
1 scant cup boiling water,
1 cup roasted peanuts,
¼ teaspoon soda.

Melt all together over a slow fire; cook gently without stirring until a little hardens when dropped in cold water; add the nuts; turn the mixture into buttered pans and cut while hot. Stirring will cause the syrup to sugar.

No. 84, PEANUT BRITTLE NUMBER TWO

2 cups granulated sugar,
1 cup freshly-roasted peanuts.

Shell and clean the peanuts; put in the stove to heat; put sugar in frying pan, and heat over a hot fire until it is changed to caramel; put the peanuts in a well-buttered tin; pour the sugar over them at once; when cold turn the pan up-side down, and tap bottom until the candy falls out: break into small pieces.

No. 85, PEANUT AND POPCORN BALLS

½ teaspoon soda,
1 pint syrup,
2 tablespoons butter,
1 teaspoon vinegar,
3 quarts freshly-popped corn,
1 quart freshly-roasted peanuts.

Cook until the syrup hardens when a little is dropped in cold water; remove to back of stove; add the soda dissolved in a teaspoon of hot water; pour syrup over the corn and nuts, stirring until each kernel is well coated; mould into balls.

No. 86, FROSTED PEANUT FUDGE

Make a good chocolate fudge; beat until creamy; pour into a well-buttered pan of about one inch depth; when nearly hard, cover with finely-chopped fig preserves; then place in a kettle 1 cup of granulated sugar, ¼ cup water, and a pinch of cream of tartar; boil until it forms a hard ball when dropped into water; pour over the stiffly-beaten white of one egg; add one teaspoon lemon juice or extract; cover fruit with a generous layer of crushed peanuts; whip syrup until creamy; pour over the fruit; when cold cut into squares.

No. 87, PEANUT PANOCHA

2 cups brown sugar,
¾ cup cream,
1 teaspoon vanilla,
2 tablespoons butter,
1 cup chopped peanuts.

Boil all the ingredients together except the vanilla and nuts until the soft-ball stage, is reached; remove from the fire and let cool; add the vanilla and nuts; beat until creamy; turn into a buttered pan; when cool cut up into squares.

No. 88, PEANUT FRUIT ROLL

3¼ cups sugar,
1 cup cream,
One-third cup coarsely-chopped peanuts,
½ cup each of figs, dates and
  candied pineapple.

Boil sugar and cream until it reaches the soft-ball stage; pour out on a large platter, and cool; work with a wooden spoon until creamy; add the nuts and fruit; work until mass begins to stiffen; then make into a long roll, and wrap in moist towel. In an hour or more it can be sliced, and the slices wrapped in oiled paper.

No. 89, SULTANA PEANUT CARAMELS

1 cup light brown sugar,
½ cup golden corn syrup,
1 tablespoon butter,
1 teaspoon vanilla extract,
1 cup granulated sugar,
½ cup milk,
½ cup coarsely-chopped peanuts.
1 cup Sultana raisins.

Place the ingredients in a sauce-pan, and boil to the firm ball stage; remove from the fire, and flavor with the vanilla. These are especially nice when dipped in chocolate.

No. 90, NUT HONEY

....

1 pound honey,
1 pound sugar,
1 tablespoon water.

Mix and set in a vessel of hot water until melted; cook over a moderate fire until it forms a ball when a little is dropped in cold water; add one pint of crushed peanuts; flavor with lemon, cut into squares.

No. 91, PEANUT ALMOND FUDGE (VERY FINE)

....

1 cup peanuts deeply browned b
    ut not scorched. Crush or grind,
1½ cups sugar,
1 cup milk,
1 tablespoon butter,
1 teaspoon almond extract.

Brown ½ cup of sugar in a granite pan; add the milk; when the brown sugar is thoroughly dissolved add one cup of granulated sugar and the butter; boil to the soft-ball stage; flavor with the extract; add the peanuts; beat until creamy; pour into buttered tins, and mark off into squares.

No. 92, PEANUT TUTTI-FRUITTI CARAMELS

2 cups light-brown sugar,
½ cup milk,
½ cup chopped dates,
¼ cup candied pineapple,
1 cup peanuts, blanched and ground,
1 cup corn syrup,
1 tablespoon butter,
1 teaspoon lemon extract,
½ cup raisins, seeded and chopped,
½ cup preserved watermelon rind, chopped very fine,
¼ cup chopped figs.

Place all the ingredients in a sauce-pan together, and boil to the hard-ball stage; stir only enough to keep the mixture from sticking. If the double boiler is used the candy will not stick much. Remove from the fire; add the extract; pour into buttered pans, and mark off into squares.

No. 93, PEANUT HONEY PUFFS

1 cup cream,
3 cups sugar,
¼ cup honey,
1 egg (white),
1 cup ground peanuts.

Boil the cream and sugar (without stirring) until the threading stage is reached; add the honey; when syrup will make a soft-ball when dropped into cold water, remove from the fire and beat into it the well-whipped white of an egg; add the nut-meats; when firm and creamy whip into balls.

No. 94, PEANUT MAPLE-SUGAR FUDGE

2 cups maple sugar,
1 cup milk,
1 cup chopped peanuts,
1 tablespoon butter.

Boil the sugar, milk, and butter to a soft-ball stage when tested in cold water; add the nut-meats; remove from the fire, and stir until creamy; pour into buttered pans; when cool cut into squares.

No. 95, PEANUT CARROT FUDGE

1 cup carrot pulp,
1 cup corn syrup,
½ cup peanut meal,
1 teaspoon vanilla or
    almond extract,
2 cups sugar,
1 tablespoon butter,
1 lemon,
1 orange.

Bake some nice, yellow carrots until tender; pass through a sieve; to a cupful of this pulp add all the ingredients except the extract; pour into buttered pans, and when cool cut into cubes; use both the juice and half the grated peel of the lemon and orange.

No. 96, PEANUT AND FIG CANDY

1 pound sugar,
½ teaspoon vinegar,
½ pint water,
½ pint chopped peanut meats.

Boil over a slow fire the sugar, water, and vinegar until it forms a hard ball when tested; stir a few times; shred the same quantity of dried figs as peanuts; mix with the peanuts; spread out in a well-buttered dish; pour the hot syrup over them; cool, and cut or break into small pieces.

No. 97, PEANUT NOUGAT

1 cup peanut meal,
1/8 teaspoon salt,
1 cup granulated sugar.

Put sugar in frying pan; stir over a slow fire; when melted add the peanut meal; mix thoroughly; butter knives and the under-side of a pan; sprinkle generously with whole and half nuts roasted to a delicate brown; shape into squares ½ inch thick. Arrange it so that each square contains one or two whole or half nuts.

No. 98, PEANUT MARSHMALLOWS

....

½ pound gum Arabic dissolved
  in 1 pint of water,
½ pound granulated sugar,
4 egg whites, well beaten,
Lemon flavoring to taste,
½ cup peanut meal,

Strain the gum Arabic; add the sugar; stir over a slow fire until dissolved; cook to the consistency of thick honey; remove from the fire, and stir in the egg whites; stir until it is somewhat thin and does no adhere to the fingers; add the lemon; pour in tins dusted with corn starch; put in cool place; when firm cut into small squares.

No. 99, PEANUT TAFFY CANDY

....

1 cup sugar,
½ cup molasses,
¼ cup butter,
1 cup peanuts (freshly-roasted peanuts—rolled).

Boil the sugar, molasses and butter together until it snaps when dropped in cold water; remove from fire; stir in the mashed pear, its; pour in buttered dish; pull when cold enough.

No. 100, PEANUT BROWNIES

1 cup sugar,
½ cup flour,
½ cup melted butter,
½ cup coarsely-ground peanuts,
2 eggs,
2 squares chocolate.

Mix and bake in shallow pan in a quick oven; garnish the top with nuts; cut in squares.

FANCY CHEESE FOR THE HOME

CREAM CHEESE (AFTER M. R. TOLSTRUP).

Into a gallon of 10% to 15% sweet cream put one or two tablespoons starter, fresh buttermilk, or clean clabbered milk; stir gently, and heat to about 85 degrees Fahrenheit. Then add about 20 drops of rennet extract or its equivalent in rennet tablets. Dilute the rennet with cold water at least 10 times its own volume before it is added to the cream. Mix well in the cream; cover up carefully so as to retain the heat; set aside for about three hours, when a soft curd will be formed. Spread a piece of cheese-cloth over a bowl, and carefully dip the curd into it; let drain for a few minutes; tie ends of the cloth together, and hang up to drain, which will require from 12 to 24 hours. Do not shake or break the curd any more than is necessary, or much fat will be lost.

When sufficiently drained salt to taste. Mix well; wrap cloth around the cheese, put between two boards, and press lightly for a few hours. When it assumes a slightly mealy consistency it is ready to eat.

If this cheese is to be marketed it must be put in glasses or 4-ounce packages, and wrapped in wax paper and tin foil, or it may be put in small 4 or 8-ounce paraffin-paper boxes.

No. 101, PEANUT CREAM CHEESE WITH OLIVES

Remove the seed and mince one ounce of olives very fine; run through a meat-mincer, and one ounce of peanuts freshly roasted and treated in the same way. To every pound of cheese add this olive and nut mixture. This is very dainty and appetizing.

No. 102, PEANUT CREAM CHEESE WITH PIMENTO

To every pound of cream cheese grind ½ ounce of pimento pepper and one ounce of peanuts in the same way as recommended for the above.

No. 103, PEANUT SANDWICH CHEESE

To each pound of cream cheese add two ounces of peanut meal; blend thoroughly.

No. 104, PEANUT COFFEE

....

½ cup peanuts,
½ cup wheat or rye,
½ cup cow peas.

Roast all to a rich coffee brown; grind and make as for postum.

To those who like a cereal coffee, this will be quite acceptable, even delicious. To more or less habitual coffee-drinkers, one-third or one-half real coffee will make the above recipe more acceptable.

No. 105, SALTED PEANUTS

....

Parch, rub, and winnow out the brown hulls; put in pan with just a speck of butter; heat gently, shaking all the time; when buttered sprinkle over with fine salt.

The above recipes are only a few of the many ways in which this wholesome pea can be prepared for human consumption. Let us hope that Macon County will seize her splendid opportunity, and that every farmer will put in at least a small acreage of peanuts.